Railways & Recollectio[ns]
Birmingham Snow Hill to Che[ltenham]
The North Warwickshire Line and
the Gloucestershire Warwickshire Railway

John Whitehouse

Contents

© John Whitehouse 2017

First published in 2017

British Library Cataloguing in Publication Data

A catalogue record for this book is available from the British Library.

Acknowledgements

My thanks go to the many people who have helped in the preparation of this book. Particular thanks go to Mrs Anne Boynton, for making available the photographic collection of her late husband, John Boynton (JB), a particularly fine author whose book *Shakespeare's Railway* (Mid England Books, ISBN 0 9522248-1-X) is essential reading. The support of Anthony Bowles (AB) of the Restoration and Archive Trust (RAT) is gratefully acknowledged for the supply of excellent archive photographs, not only from his own camera but also that of John Dagley Morris (JDM), all culled from the Trust's archive. As always Geoff Dowling (GD) has provided his stalwart support, not only from his own photographic collection, but also as joint custodian of the excellent work of the late Peter Shoesmith (PS). Grateful thanks are also due to Paul Dorney (PD), Brian Morrison (BM), Norman Preedy (NP), John Stretton (JS), Steve Widdowson (SW) and David C. Williams (DCW) for their invaluable photographic contributions, Ian Crowder of the Gloucestershire Warwickshire Railway, and finally, but not least, to Richard Tuplin, who volunteered for the unenviable job of proofreading the text and who, when last heard of, was recovering quite well!

Silver Link Publishing Ltd
The Trundle
Ringstead Road
Great Addington
Kettering
Northants NN14 4BW
Tel/Fax: 01536 330588
email: silverlinkpublishing@btconnect.com
Website: www.nostalgiacollection.com
Printed and bound in the Czech Republic

ISBN 978 1 85794 510 2

About the author

John Whitehouse believes that he was about four years old when first introduced to the lure of railways, after his grandfather took him to 'see the trains' at Milford & Brocton on the Trent Valley line. This may also explain his preference for all things 'Stanier', particularly 'The Big 'Uns' as Crewe men used to call the 'Princess Coronation' Class. However, it was not until 1974 that he took up railway photography seriously, primed by the impending demise of the diesel-hydraulic locomotives of the Western Region. The pursuit of trains on film resulted in becoming a co-author of four Nostalgia Collection 'Past & Present' titles with Geoff Dowling, and later into railway journalism with *Railway World* and *Railways Illustrated* printed magazines and now the internet-based *Railway Herald*.

Title page **BIRMINGHAM SNOW HILL**
The current Snow Hill station is surrounded by the modern tower blocks of Birmingham's business quarter, and while above the platforms there is currently car-parking space on three levels, the potential of using this area to add further valuable office space must be compelling. However, a completely new station contained within a brand-new development cannot be discounted. On 22 October 2015 Direct Rail Services Class 68 No 68008 *Avenger* awaits departure with a lunchtime service to London Marylebone. *JW*

Introduction

In 1908 the Great Western Railway opened a new through route connecting Cheltenham Spa and Birmingham. It was the amalgamation of four separate railways, which had opened incrementally from 1860, that formed this new line, arguably the last new main line until the opening of the Channel Tunnel Rail Link (later to became part of High Speed 1) in 2003. Built for the use of both fast express and suburban commuter services, it also provided the Great Western with much sought-after independence from the Midland Railway, as it no longer had to exercise running rights over its arch-rival from Birmingham to Gloucester, via the Lickey Incline.

Stratford-upon-Avon was a pivotal point of the new route. Arguably a railway town since 1826, when a tramway was constructed to link it with Moreton-in-Marsh, the first standard gauge line arrived in 1859 when the Oxford, Worcester & Wolverhampton Railway opened a branch from its Cotswold Line station at Honeybourne. A year later the Stratford-upon-Avon Railway Company completed a branch from Hatton, on the Great Western's London to Birmingham main line. Each branch initially had separate stations, less than a mile apart, and the logical outcome of connecting the two systems was completed in 1861, which included a new station serving both lines.

Earlier, in 1840, the Midland Railway had extended to Cheltenham and opened its station, known as Lansdown Road. Seven years later the Cheltenham & Great Western Union Railway, later absorbed into the Great Western Railway, extended into Cheltenham from Swindon and established another station, which was more conveniently positioned for the town centre. This closed in 1894, and a further station opened nearby; originally named just 'Cheltenham', it was expanded to Cheltenham St James in 1908 as a way of differentiating it from the new Malvern Road station that opened on the new route to Honeybourne the same year.

As the end of the 19th century approached the Great Western Railway was anxious to establish its own strategic route from the West Midlands to the West of England. By using the section of its existing network from Birmingham to Honeybourne, via Hatton and Stratford-upon-Avon, the extended route was completed by the new line south from Honeybourne to Cheltenham Spa. Surveyed with easy gradients and long curves, it would allow the GWR to facilitate fast running and higher speeds for its services on the Gloucester-Bristol-South Wales-South West axis. The first section opened between Honeybourne and Broadway on 1 August 1904, and was then extended incrementally to Cheltenham Spa (Lansdown Junction) on 1 August 1906.

Honeybourne station was served by a loop off the new main line, which not only offered a through route from Cheltenham Spa to Stratford-upon-Avon, but also to London by way of Hatton South Junction.

While Birmingham could be reached via Hatton North Junction, a shorter route, which would have connected the Hatton to Stratford-upon-Avon branch at Bearley with the Great Western's London-Birmingham main line at Tyseley, had been approved in 1894, but the Birmingham, North Warwickshire & Stratford Railway, which proposed the scheme, did not proceed with the project. It was resurrected by the Great Western Railway, which took over the project in 1900 as it fitted in with the company's strategic plans. Construction commenced in 1905, and the line opened to freight on 9 December 1907, with passenger traffic following on 1 July 1908. In addition to becoming a key gateway to the West of England, the North Warwickshire Line also became an important commuter route, with no fewer than 13 stations in the 17 miles between Tyseley and Bearley Junction, serving primarily Birmingham.

While the main focus of this book is on the development of the new lines that created the Great Western's new strategic route, the last few miles from Tyseley to Birmingham's Snow Hill station were, and remain, crucial. Snow Hill, the chequered history of which is outlined in the first section, was at the heart of the Great Western system north from Paddington. Moor Street, too, was a key investment to meet the anticipated increased demand generated by the new North Warwickshire Line, and importantly relieve the already congested Snow Hill.

The next 50 years were largely uneventful, with just the occasional opening or closure, until

WOOD END TUNNEL The Vintage Trains' 'Shakespeare Express' heads out of Wood End Tunnel on 7 July 2013, headed by GWR 'Hall' No 4965 *Rood Ashton Hall*. Note the inscription of the opening date above the tunnel portal. JW

the effect of car ownership began to impact on both lines after the Second World War. While the North Warwickshire Line had been promoted as a commuter railway, services south of Stratford-upon-Avon catered to a rural clientele and were the first to be hit, with local services from Honeybourne to Cheltenham Malvern Road and St James being withdrawn on 7 March 1960, and intermediate stations closed. Six years later and trains serving stations between Stratford-upon-Avon and Honeybourne were withdrawn, again with the line between the two towns being closed. Stratford-upon-Avon survived, now being the terminus for trains off both the North Warwickshire Line and the route from Hatton. Honeybourne, once an important junction station, was closed in 1969 following the withdrawal of the local service on the Cotswold Line.

This was the time of the closure culture promoted by the Beeching Report; the car was king and, with the freedom to rove that it provided, who needed railways? Worryingly, British Railways seemed to have also embraced this culture, employing on occasion devious means of justifying closures. Route closure proposals published in May 1966 included the North Warwickshire Line. However, BR was about to meet its nemesis, the North Warwick Line Defence Committee. This was a highly effective group and garnered more than 1,300 objections to the proposed closure, which were submitted to the local Midlands Transport Users Consultative Committee, which agreed with the objectors in that the closure would cause 'severe hardship' to users along the line.

The recommendation to retain the line was ignored, and the Minister of Transport of the day, Richard Marsh, stated that closure would take place in May 1968 subject to an alternative bus service being provided. A licence was granted to the reluctant Birmingham & Midland Motor

Omnibus Company, better known as Midland Red, in December 1968, despite two appeals by five local authorities that the proposed bus service would be inadequate.

A further appeal by the five councils was to be heard on 3 June 1969, but BR announced that services would cease on 3 May. A hectic period followed, and an application was made to the High Court for an injunction to prevent BR withdrawing the train service. This was refused, but importantly leave was granted to take the matter to the Court of Appeal. With the clock ticking towards midnight on 2 May 1969, three judges sitting in the Court of Appeal granted the requested injunction preventing BR from withdrawing the passenger service on the grounds that the appeal scheduled for 3 June had not been heard. The judges also saw fit to criticise BR for its conduct in pursuing the closure of the line.

However, this was not to be the end of the matter. In 1984 British Rail appealed to have the injunction lifted, with the proposal that the section from Henley-in-Arden to Bearley Junction should be closed, involving the loss of one station, Wootton Wawen, with the service to Stratford-upon-Avon being diverted via Solihull and Dorridge. Needless to say, this did not go down well with the local community, and eventually BR gave up and eventually withdrew its plans.

Gradually the line began to see investment, culminating in station improvements, resignalling and the provision of new rolling stock, first with the introduction of the Class 150 'Sprinters', now replaced by the more modern Class 172 DMUs, from 2011. There are aspirational plans for a more regular steam service between Birmingham and Stratford-upon-Avon, which the promoter, Vintage Trains, hope will benefit from the increased tourism that is expected to be generated by the new High Speed 2 rail link from London.

While the North Warwickshire Line's future was being fought in the courts, the southern part of the route from Stratford-upon-Avon to Cheltenham Spa continued as a freight artery between the Midlands and South Wales, also being used as a diversionary route for passenger trains as well as regular race-day specials to Cheltenham Racecourse station, which, unlike the other stations, had not been officially closed. Indeed, there were plans to upgrade the line in the early 1970s, but all this came to an abrupt end on 25 August 1976 when a Severn Tunnel-bound freight train derailed on the approach to the site of the former Winchcombe station, inflicting significant damage to the track. Although the damage was repaired, BR decided to close the line throughout from Stratford-upon-Avon to Cheltenham Spa later that year, the only remnant being a spur from Honeybourne to the then Ministry of Defence Depot at Long Marston.

Prior to the commencement of the lifting of the track in July 1979, efforts had been made to preserve the line by the Gloucestershire Warwickshire Railway Trust, and finally, in 1981, the Trust obtained a lease for part of Toddington station yard, with the first items of rolling stock arriving soon after. A Light Railway Order was obtained in 1983, which was the signal to commence the reinstatement of the track between Broadway and Cheltenham Racecourse. This was consolidated the following year by the purchase of the 'trackbed, associated land and remaining buildings'.

The first major milestone was reached with the reopening to Winchcombe, which received its first train from Toddington on 1 March 1987 after a gap of some 28 years. Of note, work had also commenced on the rebuilding of the former Monmouth Troy station buildings on the site, which had been transported brick-by-brick to Winchcombe to replace the original building that had been flattened upon the cessation of BR services. The

heritage line continued to push south, with incremental advances over the next few years, not unlike the way the line had been originally opened some 80 years earlier. Gotherington was reached in 1997, and a symbolic laying of track at Cheltenham Racecourse in 1998 was used to publicise a major share issue to fund the 'southern extension'.

Actual completion of the southern extension took a further three years, but in November 2001 the first train since the 1970s finally worked into Cheltenham Racecourse station. The event was also used to publicise an important deal for the railway's future, with Racing Tours Limited, which wished to use the railway to bring in race-goers to the adjacent Cheltenham Race Course. This arrangement continues, to the mutual benefit of all parties.

All was going well for the heritage railway until 2008, when a landslip near Cheltenham Racecourse forced the line south of Gotherington to close, with repairs extending through to early 2009, and a bill that topped £300,000. While unknown at the time, this was a foretaste of the future, as in 2010 a second serious landslip just south of Gotherington once again closed the line south of that point, resulting in a £1 million share issue to repair the damage. Then, no sooner had the Gotherington damage been repaired when another equally serious landslip occurred at 'Chicken Curve', just north of Winchcombe, which took another £1 million to resolve.

So, in the course of just three years the

railway had to find almost £2.5 million to repair the formation of the line, since when it has raised a further £2 million-plus to fund the northwards extension from Toddington to Broadway, which is due to open on Good Friday 2018. With passengers figures increasing year on year, and their proven ability to raise funds and, importantly, stay out of debt, the future of the Gloucestershire Warwickshire Railway looks assured. And, in the background, there remains the prospect of further extensions, to Honeybourne in the north to secure a main-line connection, and possibly even southwards, closer to the centre of Cheltenham Spa.

The prospects of Honeybourne have also improved since its infamous closure in 1969. Local demand resulted in the station reopening in 1981, with just a single platform for Cotswold Line services. In 2011 the redoubling project covering part of Cotswold Line resulted in a second platform being opened, which included provision for a third platform face to accommodate future services of the Gloucestershire Warwickshire Railway should the organisation decide to push north from Broadway.

A potential future development is the reinstatement of the missing 6-mile line between Long Marston and Stratford-upon-Avon, which has already been the subject of a positive case study and is being promoted by the local Avon Rail Link.

TODDINGTON The spurs of exhaust indicate that the driver of the Winchcombe-bound DMU has just 'notched up' after the token exchange with the signalman in Toddington signal box on 22 October 2015. The operation of DMUs on the Gloucestershire Warwickshire Railway is popular with passengers, and complements the steam service to provide a vintage 1960s atmosphere on the heritage line. JW

BIRMINGHAM SNOW HILL The Great Western Railway opened its first Birmingham station in 1852, initially named simply 'Birmingham'. Prior to 1858, when the Snow Hill name was adopted, the station became Great Charles Street, then Livery Street was later added. The first station building was essentially a large shed of timber construction, which was replaced by an improved structure with an arched overall roof in 1871. This was to last for just over 30 years before being replaced by a grand station in keeping with its importance to the GWR. Work on rebuilding the station took place over a six-year period from 1906, with that building lasting until services were withdrawn in 1972. Even then the structure remained until 1977, when it was finally demolished due to being deemed unsafe. Fortunately, the land had been protected from redevelopment, and in 1987 the fourth, and current, station was constructed for the reintroduction of services through Snow Hill Tunnel from the south.

The grand third station on the Snow Hill site is seen here in March 1963, with its high roof, elegant booking hall and platform buildings. It boasted two island platforms, each nearly 1,200 feet long, with up and down centre roads, while scissors crossovers allowed two trains to occupy each half of the platform independently. The outside faces of each platform were also served by through lines, and additionally bay platforms were provided at the north end. Here, the iconic 'Blue Pullman' train awaits departure from Platform 7 for London Paddington, while a 'Cross Country' DMU (later BR Class 120) occupies Platform 6 forming a service heading for Wolverhampton. *PS*

BIRMINGHAM SNOW HILL This is the view looking towards Wolverhampton with Snow Hill North Signal Box on the left as GWR 'King' Class No 6018 *King Henry VI* arrives with the 2.40pm Birkenhead-London Paddington service on 9 May 1958. Of note are the narrow station throat and intricate trackwork. *PS*

BIRMINGHAM SNOW HILL Although having the appearance of an enclosed station, the roof at Snow Hill was open for ventilation purposes and also allowed sunlight to cascade through, as seen in this early-1960s scene as BR Standard Class 9F No 92000 passes through the middle road with a short freight, overtaking a 'Blue Pullman' set that will shortly depart for London Paddington. *PS*

BIRMINGHAM SNOW HILL This late-1963 view of the north end of Snow Hill reflects the demise of steam on the Western Region as newly introduced diesel-hydraulic 'Western' Class No D1005 *Western Venturer* awaits departure with an express for Birkenhead. This view also reflects the changing shape of Birmingham as the 1960s-style edifice of Lloyd House, HQ of West Midlands Police, which can be seen on the extreme left. *PS*

BIRMINGHAM SNOW HILL lost its main-line services in 1967 with the onset of the electrification of the New Street-Euston route. For the next five years Snow Hill was only used by local shuttle services to Wolverhampton Low Level and Langley Green. Just before final closure in 1972 a Class 122 'Bubble Car' awaits departure forming a service to all stations to Wolverhampton Low Level. *GD*

Right: **BIRMINGHAM SNOW HILL** The demolition of the old Snow Hill was followed by the use of the land on which it stood as a car park, which lasted until 1987 when a fourth station was constructed in connection with the reinstatement of services through the also reopened Snow Hill Tunnel. The provision of a car park above the new station has resulted in its interior lacking the light and ambience of the old station, as illustrated by this view taken on 29 August 2015, looking through the station from the city end, as a London Midland DMU approaches. *JW*

Below: **BIRMINGHAM SNOW HILL** In 1999 the Midland Metro light rail system, more commonly called 'the tram', was opened from Wolverhampton to Birmingham, utilising much of the trackbed of the old Great Western main line. The Birmingham terminus was placed in Snow Hill, next to the portal of the tunnel leading to Moor Street. In 2015 the light rail terminus was closed and the Midland Metro line was diverted to run through the city centre. On 29 August 2015 Spanish-built CAF 'Urbos3' tram No 21 departs with a service for Wolverhampton St Georges. *JW*

Below right: **BIRMINGHAM SNOW HILL** Looking back from St Paul's tram stop towards the 'new' Snow Hill, and the impressive cityscape, Tyseley-based 'Castle' No 5043 *Earl of Mount Edgcumbe* departs with a Vintage Trains charter train to Hereford on 28 September 2013. *JW*

Birmingham Moor Street

Right: **BIRMINGHAM MOOR STREET** The original Moor Street station, which had three platforms and extensive goods facilities, was opened on 1 July 1909 by the Great Western Railway in response to anticipated increased passenger numbers following the construction of the North Warwickshire Line. It closed in 1987 when services were restored to Snow Hill, which used a new station with two through platforms constructed next to the old one. The old station building was Grade II-listed and, after a period of neglect while out of use, was itself restored to pristine condition in 2002, although due to operational issues trains did not start using the station until 2010. Future developments include increasing the number of platforms to accommodate new services from Kings Heath and Moseley. This is a view of the old station taken the day after closure on 28 September 1987. The car park on the left is the site of the old goods shed. JW

Left: **BIRMINGHAM MOOR STREET** is an architectural gem sandwiched between the modern edifices that now dominate the city centre. On the left is the futuristic Selfridge's building, behind which is the top of the 1960s icon, The Rotunda. The Pavilions and Marks & Spencer form a backdrop behind the station, while an assortment of office blocks occupies the east side of the city. A locomotive-hauled set with its Mark 3 Driving Van Trailer (DVT) leading prepares to depart for London Marylebone on 10 August 2014, while a Class 166 DMU stands in the adjacent platform and will later work to Leamington Spa. JW

Left: **BIRMINGHAM MOOR STREET** Pictured alongside what is today the disconnected Platform 5 is Tyseley's 'Castle' No 7029 *Clun Castle* prior to heading for Stratford-upon-Avon with a private charter on 17 May 1986. The headboard, 'Mile Post 65', suggests that someone is about to get their pension, but the weather is trying its best to put a damper on the celebrations. Note that the present-day Pavilions Shopping Centre is in the early stages of construction. JW

Below left: **BIRMINGHAM MOOR STREET** The 'new' Moor Street station opened in 1987 and was later refurbished together with the 'old' one, when they were merged. The 'new' station was upgraded to a Great Western style to complement the older facility, and the finished entity contrasts well with the adjacent Bull Ring Shopping Centre. On 9 August 2009 London Midland Class 150 'Sprinter' No 150015 departs from the 'new' side of Moor Street forming a service for Stratford-upon-Avon. JW

Below: **BIRMINGHAM MOOR STREET** Looking along the original island platform of the 'old' station on 16 January 2013, Platform 5 is currently out of use and disconnected; however, plans exist for it to be returned to operation together with a new Platform 6, on the right, to accommodate additional services, while the bay platforms on the left serve Chiltern Railways workings to London Marylebone. Former Great Western 'Heavy Freight' 2-8-0 No 2885 was placed on display at the station when it reopened, but this has since been moved to Tyseley Locomotive Works for restoration. JW

Bordesley and Small Heath

Right: **BORDESLEY VIADUCT** occupies the River Rea valley between Moor Street and Bordesley stations. Built in 1852, it has 60 arches, is 2,900 feet in length and 70 feet tall at its highest point. Traffic demands resulted in it being extended to accommodate two additional running lines in 1913. On 28 May 2005 ex-LMS 'Black 5' No 45305 *Alderman A. E. Draper* crosses with a Vintage Trains excursion to Didcot. New sidings have since been added to allow the stabling of Chiltern Railways stock. *JW*

Below: **BORDESLEY** GWR 'Hall' No 5933 *Kingsway Hall* passes the old Bordesley station heading for Snow Hill on 24 April 1964. The station opened in 1855 and was extended in 1915 with the provision of two extra platforms. The Midland Railway's Camp Hill line can be seen crossing the Great Western formation in the distance. *PS*

Below right: **BORDESLEY** This panoramic view from the old Great Western Warehouse at Bordesley is looking down on the Camp Hill line in the foreground as a Central Trains-liveried Class 150 'Sprinter' heads along the former Great Western main line towards Small Heath and beyond on 28 May 2005. The remains of Bordesley station can be seen in the background, now reduced to just one island platform, devoid of canopies and served by just one 'Parliamentary' train a week. *JW*

Right: **SMALL HEATH** The view from Golden Hillock Road bridge looking towards Birmingham on 12 April 1962 shows GWR 'Prairie' 2-6-2T No 8109 approaching Small Heath station with a southbound commuter working on 12 April 1962. Note the goods yard to the right of the fourth coach, and the ghostly outline of Small Heath Viaduct in the far distance. *PS*

Below: **SMALL HEATH** Another view from the same bridge shows how much has changed significantly. Gone are the terraced houses, to be replaced in the 1980s by Small Heath Middleway, part of the city's inner ring road. A notable survivor on the right, however, is the retaining wall in the cutting. On 23 May 2015 ex-LMS 'Princess Coronation' No 46233 *Duchess of Sutherland* approaches Small Heath working a charter train bound for Oxford. *JW*

SMALL HEATH & SPARKBROOK station opened in 1863, and was later enlarged to provide two island platforms during the 1915 expansion to a four-track formation. On 12 April 1963 GWR 'Manor' Class No 7817 *Garsington Manor* arrives with a stopping service, probably bound for Stratford-upon-Avon. *PS*

SMALL HEATH A much-rationalised station survives today, now simply named 'Small Heath'. The original booking hall remains, located at road level, with platform accommodation consisting of just a draughty basic shelter, while the far platform has been out of use for many years. On 21 October 2014 Chiltern Railways Class 168 No 168005 hurries through non-stop with a Snow Hill to London Marylebone service. JW

Tyseley

TYSELEY station opened on 1 October 1906 expressly to serve the upsurge in passengers locally, as well as the anticipated increase generated by the new route to Stratford-upon-Avon, which opened two years later in 1908. As with other local stations it was provided with two island platforms, both with large canopies. However, unlike other stations on the main line, it has retained its platform buildings and canopies, as it was not rationalised, like other North Warwickshire Line stations, when the main line was downgraded. Although the platform buildings today are all shut, the station remains an impressive edifice. Harking back to the days of steam, this view shows GWR 'Hall' No 4953 *Pitchford Hall* arriving on 6 September 2009 with the afternoon return working of Vintage Trains' 'Shakespeare Express' from Stratford-upon-Avon, which runs via Dorridge and therefore uses the fast line through Platform 2. JW

Below: **TYSELEY** The view looking towards Birmingham on 3 July 1964 sees GWR 'Hall' No 7929 *Wyke Hall* arriving at Platform 3, probably with a semi-fast service to Stratford-upon-Avon or Cheltenham. Note the large goods shed on the right, which was part of an extensive freight yard situated on the up side of the main line. *PS*

Right: **TYSELEY** In a busy scene on 12 March 1955 at the London end of the station, where the North Warwickshire Line diverges to the right, shows GWR pannier tank No 8792 passing Tyseley Junction Signal Box with a local service, about to cross with a semi-fast service heading for Stratford-upon-Avon or Cheltenham Spa hauled by an unidentified GWR 'Hall Class locomotive. *PS*

Below right: **TYSELEY** A visitor from the past would not notice much change with the external appearance of Tyseley station today, as it has even retained its British Railways-era 'Tyseley Station' sign on the side of the booking hall, which straddles the station on Wharfdale Road. On 18 March 2017 London Midland Class 172 No 172331 passes non-stop forming a Stratford-upon-Avon to Stourbridge service. *JW*

Tyseley depot and locomotive works

Tyseley Depot was founded in 1908 and consisted of a roundhouse with two connected 65-foot turntables and a repair shop, known as 'The Factory'. Its allocation was mainly local passenger and freight locomotives. A diesel depot was opened in 1957, located between the steam depot and the main line, while closure of the steam depot took place between 1963 and 1968. The current Tyseley Locomotive Works occupies part of the site where the main running shed was situated and utilises the building next to the coaling stage, which also still survives. In 2014 a new annex to the coaling stage building was constructed which greatly enhances its ability to restore and overhaul locomotives.

TYSELEY DEPOT Stanier-designed LMS Class 8F No 48420 stands in front of the depot on 23 May 1959, with an unidentified Churchward-designed '4300' Class 2-6-0 for company. Note the DMU at the fuelling point of the diesel depot, which had opened two years earlier. *PS*

TYSELEY DEPOT Sunlight bathes the depot on 23 May 1959 as a cleaner energetically attends to the front buffer beam of GWR 'Prairie' 2-6-2T No 6116. Alongside are two Great Western 'Halls', Nos 4919 *Donnington Hall* and 7918 *Rhose Wood Hall*. *PS*

TYSELEY LOCOMOTIVE WORKS A new annex opened in 2014 and provides much-needed additional workspace. On 4 July 2014 the centre road is occupied with the frames of 'Jubilee' No 45596 *Bahamas* and 'Castle' No 7029 *Clun Castle*. JW

TYSELEY LOCOMOTIVE WORKS
A Great Western gallery of express passenger locomotives poses in the rain in front of the surviving turntable at Tyseley on 22 June 2013. From left to right they are GWR 'Castles' Nos 5029 *Nunney Castle* and 5043 *Earl of Mount Edgcumbe* and 'Halls' Nos 4965 *Rood Ashton Hall* and 4936 *Kinlet Hall*. JW

SPRING ROAD The first station on the newly constructed North Warwickshire Line is Spring Road Platform. Its facilities have always been 'basic', with just a variety of waiting shelters over the years, and a booking office situated at road level. In 1928 its platforms were extended to accommodate longer trains and since then the only noticeable significant change is the presence of a two-tier car park that straddles the station, constructed for the benefit of the nearby Joseph Lucas factory.

Here an unidentified GWR 'Prairie' 2-6-2T departs from the station on 12 March 1955 with a North Warwickshire Line working in the direction of Stratford-upon-Avon. Although only three-quarters of a mile from Tyseley, the station serves a concentrated area of both residential and industrial properties. The original station booking office can be seen in the background, located on the road after which the station is named. *PS*

SPRING ROAD The ghastly car park dominates the station still as London Midland Class 172 DMU No 172331 arrives with a service for Stourbridge Junction on 14 April 2017. Access to the station is by ramps leading off Spring Road; that for the northbound platform can be seen on the right. *JW*

Right: **HALL GREEN** Little more than a mile from Spring Road, this is one of the principal stations on the North Warwickshire Line. Situated just off the busy Stratford Road, its serves a large residential and industrial area. On 16 May 1964 GWR 'Hall' No 6971 *Athelhampton Hall* enters the station with a southbound semi-fast service. The substantial station building on the left reflects the station's importance, while an attractive brick-and-tile waiting room is provided for passengers heading towards Stratford-upon-Avon. *PS*

Below: **HALL GREEN** Nearly 50 years later the station remains remarkably intact, except for the loss of the waiting room on the southbound platform. It is even possible to enjoy the sight of a Great Western 'Hall' as Tyseley's No 4965 *Rood Ashton Hall* passes with the lunchtime return 'Shakespeare Express' on 7 July 2013. *JW*

Below right: **HALL GREEN** A Shirley-bound DMU passes Hall Green signal box shortly before it closed in August 1984; it was later dismantled and now stands at Winchcombe on the Gloucestershire Warwickshire Railway. The car park on the left is the site of the station goods yard, which closed in 1969. Note the Lucas building, and the top deck of the Spring Road station car park just visible in front of the three-gabled roof in the background, which is Acocks Green Bus Garage. *JW*

Right: **YARDLEY WOOD** The advert will probably provoke as many emotions as the pannier tank-hauled commuter train departing from the leafy Yardley Wood station on 12 March 1955 – many 'Brummies' will have fond memories of nights out consuming Ansells Ales, then brewed locally in Aston! Maybe the next stop for the businessman who has just alighted from the train could be his local, for a pint or two... *PS*

Below: **YARDLEY WOOD** A Tyseley Class 117 DMU enters Yardley Wood forming a service for Stratford-upon-Avon on 7 July 1978. The booking hall is at the top of the ramp leading to Highfield Road, while at platform level there is a substantial waiting room on the left serving Birmingham-bound passengers. A much less grand affair is provided for Stratford-bound passengers. *PS/JB*

SHIRLEY is another of the principal stations on the North Warwickshire Line, and until the 2000s resignalling was the terminating point for local services. Nowadays Whitlocks End performs that function. From the outset the station was provided with good facilities on each platform, connected by a standard Great Western-pattern footbridge. In 2014 this was replaced by a new step-free bridge incorporating lifts, and the older example was subsequently removed. Resignalling also resulted in the demise of the mechanical signal box.

The first picture shows the old order at Shirley as Tyseley's Class 117/1 No 51806 leads a service to Stratford-upon-Avon on 16 February 1990. A classmate has also just arrived with a Birmingham-bound service. This view from the road bridge features the old footbridge, which by this time had lost its canopy, leaving passengers exposed to the elements. It was removed when the new step-free footbridge was installed. JW

Below: **SHIRLEY** station is now dominated by the new step-free footbridge and lifts installed in 2014, and replacing the original Great Western-designed footbridge, which has been removed. Otherwise the station remains virtually complete, with the original buildings and canopies on each platform intact. On 7 August 2016 No 5043 *Earl of Mount Edgcumbe* is seen again passing with the lunchtime 'Shakespeare Express' from Stratford-upon-Avon. *JW*

Above: **SHIRLEY** The ample station buildings, with canopies intact, are well illustrated in this scene, which features Tyseley-based Class 150 'Sprinter' No 150214 preparing to depart from Birmingham as 'Castle' No 5043 *Earl of Mount Edgcumbe* arrives tender-first with the morning 'Shakespeare Express' for Stratford-upon-Avon. The date is 12 September 2010, and Shirley signal box will shortly be closed upon completion of the North Warwickshire Line resignalling project. *JW*

WHITLOCKS END station opened on 6 June 1936, and was designated a 'Halt'. However, the growth of commuter traffic resulted in the station being rebuilt in 1999 with longer platforms, and further expansion of car parking facilities followed in an effort to alleviate pressure on nearby Shirley. Following the 2011 resignalling of the North Warwickshire Line, a turn-back facility was installed so that services now terminate here instead of Shirley.

This late-1950s view shows the station when it was a quiet rural halt. Heading north with a short freight is GWR pannier tank No 9682, while just arriving is one of the recently introducedDMUs heading for Stratford-upon-Avon. *PS*

WHITLOCKS END This view illustrates well the changes that have taken place at the station over recent years. The large car park is off to the left, while the step-free ramps can be seen leading to the platforms from the roadway. On 29 May 2017 London Midland Class 172 No 172342 departs from the station as an empty stock working. *JW*

WYTHALL station has an attractive street-level booking office. Originally named 'Grimes Hill', the station has since gone through a series of naming permutations until the present simple title of 'Wythall' was adopted in 1974. That name is reflected in this scene as a Stratford-upon-Avon-bound DMU approaches on 7 August 1976. *PS/JB*

Left: **EARLSWOOD** was once a substantial station similar to Shirley, originally named 'Earlswood Lakes' but from 1974 known simply as Earlswood. It was located at the summit of the long climb from Bearley Junction, a particularly hard slog for freight workings that prompted the provision of a water crane here for locomotives. Rationalisation has been drastic over the years, as only basic shelters are now provided, and the footbridge has been removed, with passengers having to use the road bridge to change platforms. On 7 April 1958 a DMU arrives at the then named 'Earlswood Lakes' forming a service that will terminate at Henley-in-Arden. *PS/ JB*

Right: **THE LAKES** Three-quarters of a mile separates Earlswood and The Lakes stations. The Lakes Halt opened on 3 June 1935, principally to provide access to the nearby popular reservoir. Its facilities have always been basic with passenger accommodation being just a variety of shelters over the years. A notable feature is its short platforms, and the station is one of four request stops on the North Warwickshire Line, the others being Wood End, Danzey and Wootton Wawen. On 1 June 1976 a three-car Metro-Cammell-built DMU is about to depart from The Lakes forming a service for Birmingham. The guard and sole passenger seem to be exchanging greetings on a day that reflects the hot summer of that year. *PS/JB*

Right: **WOOD END** Situated just under 2 miles apart in rural Warwickshire, Wood End and Danzey both opened with the line in 1908, and both are now request stops. Wood End's location is somewhat off the beaten track, at the end of a pathway from the main road with the platforms situated at the bottom of a cutting. Since the loss of its footbridge, the only way to change platforms is by taking the long walk to the roadway, which runs over the 175-yard tunnel situated at the Stratford-upon-Avon end of the station. Originally known as Wood End Platform, its facilities have always been basic. This panoramic late-1960s view shows the position of the station within the quite deep cutting. It also provides a good impression of the distance to be walked nowadays to change platforms, following the removal of the footbridge. *PD*

Left: **DANZEY** still retains the luxury of a footbridge, but as it is of the same concrete construction as that at Wood End its days may be numbered. The station serves the nearby settlement of Tanworth-in-Arden and once boasted a decent-sized goods yard. Like Wood End, though, it has never enjoyed more than limited passenger facilities. In this view from the Danzey Green Lane bridge looking back towards the station on a wet 25 March 1965, a southbound DMU enters the station. The goods yard was situated at the far end of the station in the area just visible beyond the footbridge, and a couple of houses flank the station on the left. *PS/JB*

HENLEY-IN-ARDEN's first station opened in 1894 at the end of a branch line from Rowington Junction on the Great Western main line, but was superseded in 1908 by a station on the newly opened North Warwickshire Line. In addition to the two new through platforms, a bay platform was provided on the northbound side to accommodate terminating services. Rationalisation in later years saw the demolition of the buildings on the island platform, their replacement coming in the form of a waiting shelter. More recently a new footbridge, incorporating lifts for step-free access, has replaced the original of Great Western design, which after refurbishment is being utilised at the soon-to-be-reopened Gloucestershire Warwickshire Railway station at Broadway.

In this view from the footbridge on 4 August 1964 a single-car diesel unit departs for Birmingham. Beyond the signal box is the connection to the stub of the line to Rowington Junction, now used for sidings. The line into the bay platform is on the left and the station still has an operational water crane. The signal box was closed in 2011 and subsequently demolished. *PS/JB*

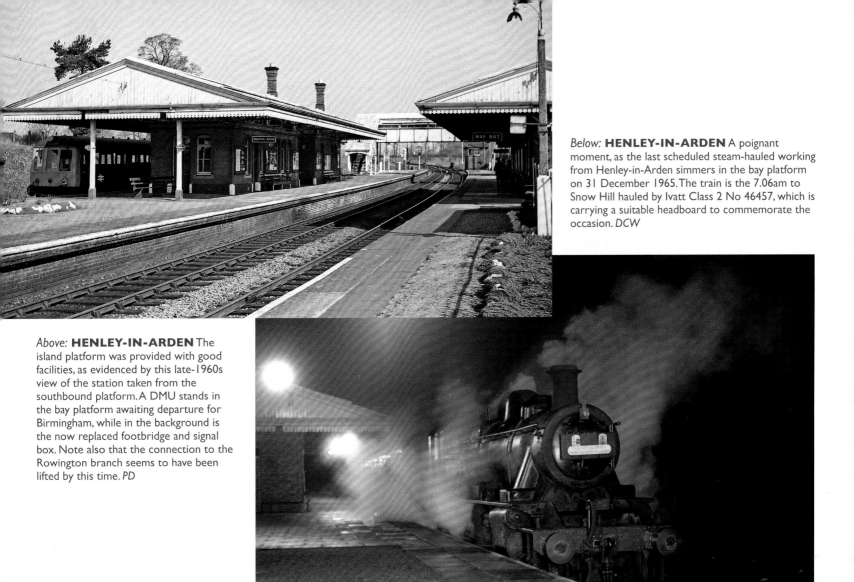

Below: **HENLEY-IN-ARDEN** A poignant moment, as the last scheduled steam-hauled working from Henley-in-Arden simmers in the bay platform on 31 December 1965. The train is the 7.06am to Snow Hill hauled by Ivatt Class 2 No 46457, which is carrying a suitable headboard to commemorate the occasion. *DCW*

Above: **HENLEY-IN-ARDEN** The island platform was provided with good facilities, as evidenced by this late-1960s view of the station taken from the southbound platform. A DMU stands in the bay platform awaiting departure for Birmingham, while in the background is the now replaced footbridge and signal box. Note also that the connection to the Rowington branch seems to have been lifted by this time. *PD*

Below: **HENLEY-IN-ARDEN** For a period while the new footbridge was being constructed a temporary replacement was erected at the south end of the station, affording an elevated view. On 15 April 2014 a pair of Class 172 DMUs calls at the station forming a service from Stratford-upon-Avon to Stourbridge Junction. Note how the span of the old footbridge, which crossed what was once the bay platform line, has been incorporated into the new step-free design. *JW*

Above: **HENLEY-IN-ARDEN** A grey day greets Class 150 'Sprinter' No 150007 as it approaches Henley-in-Arden forming a service for Stratford-upon-Avon on 17 February 2007. Although the station had been unstaffed for many years it remained looked after, as evidenced by the painted rocks that surround the running-on board. The signal box is manned and at that time had another three years of life before being rendered redundant when the route was resignalled. *JW*

Right: **WOOTTON WAWEN PLATFORM** is one of the original stations on the newly opened North Warwickshire Line, but has never enjoyed any kind of substantial facilities. Now unmanned and a request stop only, it shows little material change from when first opened, with just rudimentary waiting shelters on each platform accessed by ramps from the roadway below. On 8 April 2017 a lone cyclist has just indicated to the driver of the approaching Stourbridge Junction-bound Class 172 DMU that he wishes to join the train. *JW*

Below: **EDSTONE AQUEDUCT**, near Bearley, is the longest such structure in England. It carries the Stratford-upon-Avon Canal across a minor road, the North Warwickshire Line and the closed Alcester Railway. It also once had a facility to water steam locomotives from a pipe that led from the canal. On 19 April 2016 one of the occupants of a tourist barge is lining up a photograph of the passing London Midland Class 172 DMU as it heads for Stratford-upon-Avon. *GD*

BEARLEY JUNCTION When construction of the North Warwickshire Line was completed in 1908, the new route formed a junction, at a point just south of the Edstone Aqueduct, with the existing Alcester Railway, which had opened in 1876. A short distance further, another junction was formed with the line of the Stratford Railway from Hatton at Bearley Junction. The Alcester line continued to the north of Bearley Junction, to join the Stratford Railway at a point close to the present Bearley station, thereby forming a triangle. At one time, each junction in this layout was protected by its own signal box but, following the closure of the Alcester line in 1964, rationalisation resulted in only one signal box, that within the angle of the North Warwickshire and Hatton lines, surviving until 2010, when the area was resignalled. Just prior to the closure of the former Bearley Junction West Signal Box on 12 September 2010, GWR 'Castle' No 5043 *Earl of Mount Edgcumbe* eases around the curve off the Stratford-upon-Avon to Hatton line with Vintage Trains' 'Shakespeare Express'. *JW*

WILMCOTE is a gem of a station, exuding a Great Western heritage from every aspect. It is not the original, however, as the first station opened in 1860 with the line from Hatton to Stratford-upon-Avon. It was superseded by the current station in 1907, in anticipation of the opening of the North Warwickshire Line the following year. Nowadays it is unstaffed, but the station has retained its charm, and the main building on the northbound side retains its canopy, which is narrower than most and supported by wooden trusses positioned along the building's facia. On the southbound side there is a smaller brick-and-tile waiting shelter, while the running lines are spanned by a particularly fine Great Western-pattern footbridge.

The old order prevails in this late-1980s view of the station as a Tyseley-based Class 117 DMU approaches with a service for Stratford-upon-Avon. The notable change at Wilmcote is that the Station Road bridge has been rebuilt, and strengthened in the process, as, although a rural location, the proximity of Ann Hathaway's Cottage generates much traffic, including many tour buses. The original 1860 station was located on the other side of the road bridge. JW

WILMCOTE This view from the footbridge, with Class 172 DMU No 172343 approaching forming a service for Stourbridge Junction on 14 September 2014, illustrates the finer points of the station's architecture, a view being shared by the young lady on the platform. JW

WILMCOTE In this near timeless scene, a period Great Western station and a Great Western-built locomotive go together as easily as bread and butter. On 1 September 2013 Swindon-built 'Hall' No 4965 *Rood Ashton Hall* passes Wilmcote with the lunchtime 'Shakespeare Express' returning to Snow Hill via Dorridge. *JW*

BISHOPTON The view from the A46 road bridge at Bishopton shows the expansion of the town as a new housing development takes shape on the left. However, this 9 July 2005 scene shows an essentially rural outlook with the peace temporarily being interrupted by the passage of LMS 'Jubilee' No 5690 *Leander* working the afternoon 'Shakespeare Express' to Snow Hill. *JW*

STRATFORD-UPON-AVON PARKWAY It's all change at Bishopton ten years later as the housing development of 2005 is now a mature residential estate and a new station has been opened alongside a large area serving a 'Park and Ride' scheme. Stratford-upon-Avon Parkway opened to passengers in May 2013, and serves commuters to Birmingham and beyond. On 21 November 2016 London Midland Class 172 DMU No 172212 departs with a service for Stourbridge Junction. *JW*

STRATFORD TRAMWAY Rails first appeared in Stratford-upon-Avon in 1826 with the opening of the Stratford & Moreton Tramway, an ambitious but eventually troubled scheme. It ran from the canal basin in the town to Moreton-in-Marsh and included a branch to Shipston-on-Stour. By 1845 it had been acquired by the Oxford, Worcester & Wolverhampton Railway (OW&WR), whose successor, the Great Western Railway, converted the section from Moreton to Shipston-on-Stour into a 'proper' railway in 1889. The remainder of the tramway closed in 1902, its one remaining legacy being the bridge that straddles the canal basin in Stratford-upon-Avon. JW

Left: **STRATFORD-UPON-AVON** This view shows how the buildings on each platform were offset, with the footbridge acting as the key link. The facilities on the right remain, unlike those on the island platform (left), which have been demolished. On 6 April 1958 GWR Churchward 2-8-0 No 2883 eases a Severn Tunnel Junction-bound freight from the goods yard, which was situated between the main lines and the background gasometer. *BM*

Below: **STRATFORD-UPON-AVON** The OW&WR (affectionately known as 'The Old Worse & Worse') was also responsible for bringing the first railway as such into the town with a branch from its Oxford to Worcester main line at Honeybourne, which ran into a new station at Sanctuary Lane in 1860. A year later, the Stratford Railway completed its branch from the Great Western main line at Hatton, via Bearley, to a new station situated on the Birmingham Road. The two termini were close together and the advantage of connecting the two branches was achieved in 1861 when the 'gap' was bridged, a new station opening in July of that year. The two terminus stations closed at the same time, although Birmingham Road remained open for goods until 1968.

In early 1963 the island platform buildings and canopy are well illustrated as GWR Collett 0-6-0 No 2211 prepares to depart with the 8.43am service to Leamington Spa. Note the DMU positioned beyond at the Honeybourne end of the platform. On the right is a wartime warehouse, since demolished, the site now being occupied by a Morrisons supermarket. *AB/RAT*

STRATFORD-UPON-AVON West Signal Box was tucked in beneath the Alcester Road bridge, beyond which can be seen the outer face of the station's island platform. On 1 June 1964 GWR 'Castle' Class No 7014 *Caerhays Castle* departs southwards with the 5.43pm Birmingham Snow Hill to Worcester semi-fast service. *AB/RAT*

Left: **STRATFORD-UPON-AVON** This late-1980s view is looking north over the Stratford-upon-Avon Canal towards Stratford-upon-Avon East Signal Box, which at that time controlled the station and what remained of the goods yard. This replaced an earlier signal box that was located nearer the station. Regional Railways Class 150 'Sprinter' No 150122 approaches forming a working from Birmingham. *JW*

Below left: **STRATFORD-UPON-AVON** In 1976 the line south of Stratford-upon-Avon to Cheltenham closed following a derailment to the south at Winchcombe. Nowadays just a short headshunt extends beyond the station to permit locomotives to run round their trains. Little more than a year before the enforced closure of the line, a rare passenger working traversed the route in the form of a Plymouth to Derby rail tour hauled by 'Western' No 1052 *Western Viceroy*, which is seen approaching Stratford-upon-Avon on 29 March 1975. *JW*

Below: **STRATFORD-UPON-AVON** In order to provide step-free access to the island platform, a new footbridge incorporating lifts was installed in 2015, although unusually the existing Great Western-designed structure was retained. The two bridges stand side by side, as illustrated here, with Chiltern Railways Class 165 'Turbo' No 165024 standing in Platform 2 forming a local service to Leamington Spa on 8 April 2017. *JW*

Stratford-upon-Avon to Honeybourne

Although part of the through route from Stratford-upon-Avon to Cheltenham Spa, the section to Honeybourne reflected its origins as a branch off the Cotswold Line. Passenger services operated via Honeybourne and the Cotswold Line to Worcester, although these were withdrawn in 1966. Local services over the route south to Cheltenham Spa were primarily a separate concern,

although in the latter years the line was principally used by freight services with just the occasional race-day special to Cheltenham Racecourse station. Its final demise was brought about as a result of the damage caused by the Winchcombe derailment in 1976.

South of Stratford-upon-Avon there were a number of stations, commencing with Evesham

Road Crossing, which closed in 1916, Sancta Lane, the original terminus of the line from Honeybourne that closed in 1861 when the through route was established, Racecourse Platform and Chambers Crossing; both the latter were closed as a wartime economy measure in 1916. These were followed by perhaps the two most substantial stations on the line, Milcote and Long Marston, both of which closed

in 1966. A further two halts filled the gap between Long Marston and Honeybourne, these being Pebworth, a survivor through to 1966, and nearby Broad Marston, which was another casualty of wartime economy measures, being the third closure in 1916.

A short section of the line remains open northwards from Honeybourne to serve the former Ministry of Defence establishment at Long Marston, situated just behind the station, which is now in private ownership and used for a variety of railway-related purposes including rolling stock storage.

Opposite page: **STANNALS BRIDGE** is just south of Stratford-upon-Avon Racecourse, and carries the railway across the River Avon. It is a substantial girder-type construction, seen here in the background as GWR 'Modified Hall' No 7929 *Wyke Hall* heads a Birmingham Snow Hill to Worcester Shrub Hill working in May 1964. The bridge remains today as part of the Stratford Greenway cycle route, which follows the trackbed of the line. *AB/RAT*

Below: **MILCOTE** On 18 April 1964 'Merchant Navy' Class No 35011 *General Steam Navigation* hurries through Milcote with a returning theatre special from Stratford-upon-Avon to Oxford and beyond. This was the second station at Milcote, dating from 1908 when the route was doubled and replacing the original station that was situated on the far side of the level crossing and consisted of just a single platform. *AB/RAT*

Right: **LONG MARSTON** Two years before closure, Long Marston station looks pristine and in excellent repair as a three-car DMU approaches forming a service heading for Worcester via Honeybourne on 4 August 1964. *PS/JB*

Below: **LONG MARSTON** By 23 January 1988 the station site has been flattened and is now an industrial estate, but the old station remained for some time after closure as confirmed by this view. *SW*

Below right: **LONG MARSTON DEPOT** is situated at the rear of the station site, on the east side. The course of the old trackbed can clearly be identified on the left as Class 37/0 No 37170 departs from the depot on 24 April 1987. Of note is the resident shunting locomotive on the right with a rake of wagons. *SW*

Honeybourne has something of a chequered history. The Oxford, Worcester & Wolverhampton Railway first established a station there in 1853, and its importance was enhanced when the same company opened the branch to Stratford-upon-Avon in 1860. The creation of the new line from Cheltenham Spa in 1904 consolidated the station's importance as a junction and, although the new through route avoided the station, a West Loop was created to connect with it. Although principally serving Cotswold Line trains, the new through line also created an East Loop for Stratford-upon-Avon services and a South Loop that avoided the station, giving trains from Stratford-upon-Avon eastbound access to the Cotswold Line. However, the loss of passenger services from both Cheltenham Spa in 1960 and Stratford-upon-Avon in 1966 diluted Honeybourne's importance, and the final ignominy came in 1969 when the station closed following the withdrawal of the stopping services on the Cotswold Line.

All was not lost, however, and local factors generated enough support for the station to be reopened in 1981, just as a single platform. But the Network Rail Cotswold Line redoubling project reinstated an island platform in 2011, initially only with one face for services, but including the provision for a potential third face to be added to accommodate any future services off the Gloucestershire Warwickshire Railway.

HONEYBOURNE In its heyday the station spanned two sets of double tracks served by four platforms, two outer and one island. All were accessed by a footbridge that spanned all four running lines, seen in this view taken on 4 August 1964 as Collett 0-6-0 No 2222 works 'light engine' through the station in the direction of Stratford-upon-Avon. *PS*

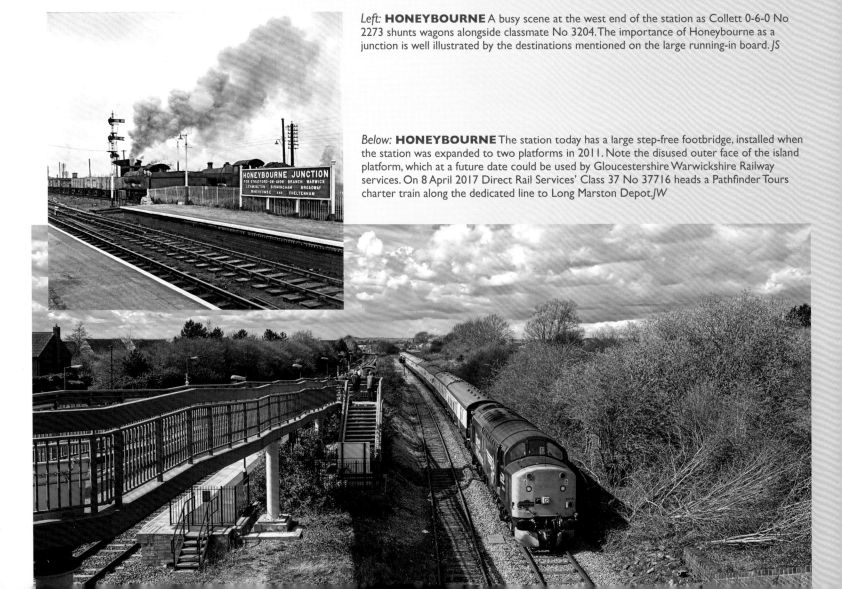

Left: **HONEYBOURNE** A busy scene at the west end of the station as Collett 0-6-0 No 2273 shunts wagons alongside classmate No 3204. The importance of Honeybourne as a junction is well illustrated by the destinations mentioned on the large running-in board. *JS*

Below: **HONEYBOURNE** The station today has a large step-free footbridge, installed when the station was expanded to two platforms in 2011. Note the disused outer face of the island platform, which at a future date could be used by Gloucestershire Warwickshire Railway services. On 8 April 2017 Direct Rail Services' Class 37 No 37716 heads a Pathfinder Tours charter train along the dedicated line to Long Marston Depot. *JW*

Right: **BROADWAY** The line south from Honeybourne to Cheltenham Spa was opened incrementally from 1904 to 1906. The section to Broadway opened first in August 1904, together with the station, which is situated around a mile from the centre of the village that has since become a popular tourist attraction. Closure came in March 1960, upon withdrawal of the local passenger service. This view dates back to the opening of the station, with building materials still piled on the platform, contrasting with the ladies in their elegant Edwardian gowns. *AB/RAT*

Below: **BROADWAY** Passenger services used a variety of Great Western traction over the years, ranging from railmotors – essentially steam-driven carriages – through to pannier tanks and auto-trains. This view shows a push-pull-fitted GWR '1400' Class 0-4-2T, about to depart for Honeybourne. *JDM/RAT*

Right: **BROADWAY**'s station buildings were demolished following the withdrawal of the passenger service, as can be seen from this view as a rake of mineral wagons forming the 8.20am Cheltenham-Honeybourne pick-up freight and hauled by pannier tank No 3616 passes the station site on 19 March 1965. Station Drive can be seen on the left. *JDM/RAT*

BROADWAY A vision of the future as the construction of a new station approaches an intermediate stage in September 2016. It will become the northern terminus of the Gloucestershire Warwickshire Railway's line from Cheltenham Racecourse, built with the aid of a successful £1.5 million share offer to fund the entire Broadway Extension project. A grand opening is planned for Good Friday 2018. This is the view looking north with the bridge over the B4362 in the foreground. The original signal box stood next to the bridge on the right, while the new box is positioned on the platform. Extensive renovation work has been necessary to bring the footbridge, previously from Henley-in-Arden, up to scratch. Excellent facilities will be offered in the new station building, now under construction on the southbound platform, which will incorporate a booking office, shop and refreshment room. *JW*

Left: **LAVERTON HALT** The original double-track alignment is clearly evident from this September 2016 view through the cab window of a GWR DMU heading for the site of Laverton Halt, which is just beyond the distant second bridge. The halt was opened in 1905 and closed in 1960, and nothing remains today. The nearer bridge carries the B4362 Toddington-Broadway road over the railway. *JW*

Below: **STANWAY VIADUCT** The most notable feature along the route is the 15-arch Stanway Viaduct, located around a mile north of Toddington; it is 210 yards long and 50 feet tall at its highest point. It was opened with the line in 1904, but not before a disaster had overcome its construction when two arches collapsed without warning on Friday 13 November 1903, killing four workmen. The structure both looks and remains very solid as 'Manor' Class No 7820 *Dinmore Manor* crosses with a southbound working on 3 April 2014. *JW*

Right: **TODDINGTON** station opened on 1 December 1904, when the section from Broadway was completed. It was then, and for all its service life until closure on 7 March 1960, just an intermediate station on the line. The goods yard remained until 1967, when it too was closed. However, even beyond the total closure of the line in 1976 the station buildings, signal box and goods shed were not demolished, and were to become a great asset to the preservationists when they took over the site in 1981. Now, of course, not only has the station been restored to its former glory but is also the headquarters of the Gloucestershire Warwickshire Railway.

On 29 August 1962 GWR 'Hall' No 6984 *Owsden Hall* heads south through Toddington with a Crewe to Bristol freight. Although having been closed for two years, the station looks in a reasonable state of repair, and the connection to the goods yard remains intact as the facility continued until 1967 to deal with the seasonal crops of the local fruit-growing industry. *JDM/RAT*

Left: **TODDINGTON** Desolation in December 1979 as contractors for British Rail are in the process of lifting the track from the now closed line. Note, though, that the station buildings and what remains of both platforms remain, as does the signal box and goods shed. Their ultimate survival became a significant asset to the newly formed Gloucestershire Warwickshire Railway. *AB/RAT*

TODDINGTON Pure Great Western heritage at Toddington on 24 May 2010. The station building is the original dating back to when the line first opened in 1904, as is the water tower on the right, while the footbridge is a recent addition installed by the Gloucestershire Warwickshire Railway. However, the main feature here is the presence of the sole surviving member of the Great Western's '3700' or 'City' Class' 4-4-0 No 3717 *City of Truro*, which in 1904 is claimed to have been the first locomotive to achieve the landmark 100mph when descending Wellington Bank in Somerset while working an 'Ocean Mails' special from Plymouth to London Paddington. Alongside is '4500' Class 2-6-2T No 5542. The occasion was to mark the extension north from Toddington across Stanway Viaduct. JW

Above: **TODDINGTON** A number of the original buildings at Toddington survived closure, as seen in this July 2012 view. The station buildings on both platforms are the originals, as is the signal box and the goods shed behind the camera, the latter now used by the Locomotive Department. Standing in the platform is Class 122 'Bubble Car' No 55003, which was built in 1958 by the nearby Gloucester Railway Carriage & Wagon Company. *JW*

Top right: **TODDINGTON** Situated at the rear of the station car park is a little gem, the North Gloucestershire Railway, a 2-foot narrow-gauge system; previously the Dowty Railway Preservation Society, it moved to Toddington in 1985. On 11 September 2016 No 6 *Chakas Kraal* departs from the main station for the terminus at Toddington. The locomotive was built by the Hunslet Engine Company of Leeds, but spent its working life in South Africa, hence its name. *JW*

Right: **HAYLES ABBEY HALT** was established by the Great Western in 1928, primarily to serve the museum at nearby Hailes Abbey (note the different spelling). It was only ever a basic affair constructed from redundant railway sleepers, and it closed on 7 March 1960. All trace of the station was subsequently removed, but the heritage line is now in the process of re-opening it, and in so doing replicating the design of the original corrugated waiting shelter. On 22 April 2017 Churchward 2-8-0T No 4270 passes the new station, which was formally reopened a few weeks later on 5 June. *JW*

The piecemeal extension of the line from Honeybourne reached Winchcombe on 1 February 1905, when both passenger and goods services commenced. Together with the other intermediate stations, Winchcombe closed on 7 March 1960, although goods traffic survived for a further four years. The station did not fare as well as Toddington thereafter, however, as the buildings and signal box were demolished before the eventual closure of the line in 1976, with just the goods shed surviving. From that low point, Winchcombe's fortunes have improved, first by the heritage Gloucestershire Warwickshire Railway being granted a lease of the trackbed by British Rail in 1981, followed by its outright purchase of the trackbed three years later. Subsequently, in 1986 the station building from Monmouth Troy was transported to Winchcombe brick by brick and reassembled on the site, in time for services from Toddington to commence in 1987. In a similar fashion, the signal box from Hall Green was also transferred to the site and rebuilt, and now controls the station area. The goods shed has also been extended at both ends to form a carriage maintenance and repair facility.

WINCHCOMBE There seems to be some rush to get aboard the 9.40am Honeybourne to Cheltenham Spa St James service at Winchcombe on 7 March 1960, perhaps due to it being the last day of passenger operations on the line. Note how well-kept the station is even though closure and subsequent demolition are nigh. *JS*

Above: **WINCHCOMBE** In the desolation that followed total closure of the line, all that remains in this view looking towards Cheltenham is the old goods shed. All the station buildings and platforms were demolished in 1965, as was the original signal box, which had remained open to deal with the goods traffic until that ceased in 1964. The 1976 derailment, which led to the closure of the line, occurred close to this point. *AB/RAT*

Right: **WINCHCOMBE** This is the revitalised scene at Winchcombe on 24 August 1991, four years after reopening by the Gloucestershire Warwickshire Railway. The surviving goods shed can be seen in the left background, next to the new signal box, which was removed brick-by-brick from Hall Green (see page 20). Behind the trees on the right there is a glimpse of the new station building, although not quite so new, as it formerly stood at Monmouth Troy. What will become the station loop is being used as a siding, and the footbridge is still to be erected as visiting GWR 'Castle' No 5080 *Defiant* enters the station with a service from Toddington. *JW*

WINCHCOMBE At the 'new' station under the ownership of the Gloucestershire Warwickshire Railway in April 2014 GWR 'Manor' Class 4-6-0 No 7820 *Dinmore Manor* simmers in the platform. A new footbridge has now been erected giving access to Platform 2, where a waiting room has been erected. The former Monmouth Troy station building has now acquired an impressive canopy, while in the background the old goods shed has been extended and now accommodates the railway's Carriage & Wagon workshops. *JW*

GREET TUNNEL is just south of Winchcombe. Some 693 yards in length, it is the second major engineering feature on the line. Gretton Halt was situated just south of the tunnel, opening in 1906 and surviving through to 1960. On 16 May 2015 former Southern Railway Bulleid 'Merchant Navy' No 35006 *Peninsular & Oriental S.N. Co* emerges from the northern portal of the tunnel on its inaugural day in traffic, which was the culmination of a 33-year restoration project. *JW*

DIXTON CUTTING On the approach to Gotherington the line runs through Dixton Cutting, where British Railways Type 1 (later Class 20) No D8137 is seen approaching with a train from Laverton on 29 December 2015. Attached to the rear is GWR 'Prairie' No 5542, which will later return the train north. *JW*

Gotherington station opened on 1 June 1906, but closed on 13th June 1955, some five years prior to the withdrawal of the passenger service. The station house survived demolition, and is today a private residence whose current owner Bryan Nicholls has maintained a railway theme as well as producing an earlier volume in this series (No. 39 Gotherington Station).

Above: **GOTHERINGTON** Bryan Nicholls, who owns Gotherington station house, has set up a wonderful array of former Great Western artefacts and structures in his garden, which was once the station's goods yard. Notable is a 'Pagoda' shelter and the 'Gotherington Halt' running-in board. It is open to the public on certain days each year. *JW*

Left: **GOTHERINGTON** Passengers wait on the GWR platform for the arrival of Class 37 No 37219, which is sitting in Gotherington Loop awaiting permission to proceed with a train from Cheltenham Racecourse to Toddington on 29 December 2015. *JW*

GOTHERINGTON station has to be one of the most attractive in the country, as it just oozes Great Western heritage. However, on 29 December 2015 it is Class 45/1 'Peak' No 45149 that is grabbing the attention of the photographers as it leads GWR 'Manor' No 7820 *Dinmore Manor* on a service from Toddington to Cheltenham Racecourse. *JW*

BISHOPS CLEEVE Viewed from the end of the station platform, the signalman watches the passing of GWR 'Grange' No 6819 *Highnam Grange* as it works north with a Cardiff to Birmingham Snow Hill express on 16 August 1958. Of note is the signal box, which unusually is built from Cotswold stone instead of the more normal red brick. *JS*

BISHOPS CLEEVE station was situated just to the north of the goods yard and was accessed from Station Road, which is situated roughly at the end of this freight train, being hauled by GWR 'Manor' No 7812 *Erlestoke Manor* on 30 May 2016. Like most other stations on the line, it opened on 1 August 1905 and was closed on 7 March 1960, and like Winchcombe was demolished; a residential development now occupies the site. *JW*

SOUTHAM ROAD

Cheltenham is world-famous for horse-racing, and the annual Gold Cup in particular. Racing in the area dates back to 1815, and was centred at Prestbury Park, the location of the present-day racecourse, in 1831. Cheltenham Racecourse station was opened by the Great Western in 1912, six years after the line opened, specifically to cater for race-day traffic. It continued to do so up to the time the line was closed in 1976, with the last trains serving the Gold Cup meeting in March of that year. It reopened in 2003, and in so doing became the southern terminus of the Gloucestershire Warwickshire Railway. This view shows the prominent position of the racecourse in the background as Class 9F No 92203 *Black Prince*, which was at the time owned by famous wildlife and railway artist David Shepherd, approaches Southam Road bridge, having just left the Racecourse station with a service for Toddington on 28 August 2008. JW

Right: **CHELTENHAM RACECOURSE** Unkempt and overgrown, the station still boasts the 'Cheltenham Race Course' running-in board on 24 July 1968. Note that the Great Western described it as 'Race Course' whereas the Gloucestershire Warwickshire Railway calls it 'Racecourse'. A sole figure wanders along the specially extended 14-coach platforms, so built to cater for race-day specials. The main A435 road bridge can be seen in the background, and through its arch is the portal of Hunting Butts Tunnel. *JS*

Below right: **CHELTENHAM RACECOURSE** A 'Spooky Special' has just arrived at Cheltenham Racecourse on 31 October 2015, in celebration of Halloween, hauled by GWR 'Prairie' No 5542. To the right is the ramp that leads to the road-level booking office, while volunteers can be seen working on the restoration of the second platform. *JW*

Below: **CHELTENHAM RACECOURSE** station booking office is located at road level, although access can only be gained via the racecourse. It is the only surviving example of the Great Western's use of prefabricated sections, which were then transported to their location by rail and assembled on site. Having survived the years of neglect, it has now been extensively refurbished by the heritage railway. *JW*

Left: **CHELTENHAM RACECOURSE** This panoramic view of the station, looking from the A435 road bridge on 30 May 2016, shows GWR 'Manor' No 7820 *Dinmore Manor* arriving with a service from Toddington, and GWR 'Hall' No 7903 *Foremarke Hall* waiting at Platform 2 in readiness to work the train back north. The station is now fully signalled following the commissioning of the new Cotswold-stone-clad signal box in 2003. *JW*

Right: **CHELTENHAM RACECOURSE** The end of the line: this is the southern terminus of the Gloucestershire Warwickshire Railway, and on 3 April 2014 after taking water 'Manor' No 7820 *Dinmore Manor* will detach and run round its train prior to working back to Toddington. *JW*

Cheltenham Spa stations

Three stations within Cheltenham Spa served trains on the line to Honeybourne – St James, Malvern Road and High Street Halt. St James was a terminus station that opened in 1894, replacing the first station in the town that had opened in 1847 on a nearby site. In addition to Great Western services to Swindon and beyond, it also served Honeybourne line trains until Malvern Road opened in 1908. The opening of Malvern Road, located just to the south of the junction for St James, catered for the new through services from Birmingham after the opening of the North Warwickshire Line, with then just a shuttle connection serving St James. The third station was High Street Halt, not to be confused with a similarly named station, lacking the 'Halt' designation, on the nearby Midland main line. Although there were plans for a larger station, they did not materialise and it remained just a halt from opening in 1908 to its early closure as a wartime economy measure in 1917.

CHELTENHAM ST JAMES This is the view looking into the station with the spire of St Gregory's RC Church in the background. Former Southern Railway Maunsell-designed 'U' Class No 31791 awaits departure while a more modern DMU stands in the adjacent platform. Note the goods shed on the extreme right, which dealt with a wide range of goods, including livestock. *AB/RAT*

Above: **CHELTENHAM MALVERN ROAD** Looking south from the road bridge that straddled the station throat, we see the island platform, an unusual feature for the line, as well as the station buildings. The engine shed is located just off the picture at the top right. *JS*

Right: **CHELTENHAM MALVERN ROAD** Looking north on 29 August 1964, 'Castle' No 5056 *Earl of Powis* has the road to continue with an express. Note the distinctive Malvern Road bridge in the background and the distant signal box that controlled the junction to St James. *JS*

CHELTENHAM LANSDOWN JUNCTION Looking north, the Midland main line curves off to the left and the Great Western route to Honeybourne proceeds straight ahead, the junction protected by an impressive signal gantry. South of here there was a four-track formation, which carried both Great Western and Midland services. On 12 March 1959 Maunsell-designed 'U' Class No 31620 approaches from the Midland's Lansdown station on a service via the old Midland & South West Junction Railway to Southampton. *NP*

Front cover: **WINCHCOMBE** The driver and fireman of GWR 'Manor' No 7820 *Dinmore Manor* enjoy a well-earned break at Winchcombe on 3 April 2014 as they chat to the guard on the platform. It has been a busy morning for all, as their train was involved in a photographers' charter on the Gloucestershire Warwickshire Railway, and an equally busy afternoon lies ahead. *JW*